No Extras

We're all going camping with Dad,
and we're only allowed to take
what's absolutely necessary.
NO EXTRAS!

I'm going camping with Dad,
and I'm only taking ...

my sleeping bag.

I'm only taking ...

my sleeping bag
and my fishing gear.

I'm only taking
my sleeping bag,
my fishing gear,

and my flashlight.

Hold it!
I've changed my mind.

I'm taking my air mattress, too.

Well then ...

I'm taking my boots, too.

Well then ...

I'm taking my hat, too.

Hold it!
I said we're only taking what's
absolutely necessary,
NO EXTRAS!

STAGE 3

SET A

Wrinkles
Talk, Talk, Talk
March Along with Me
Bruno's Birthday
Legs
Riddles
Sleeping
Monkey's Friends

SET B

At Night
Secret Soup
Moonlight
Bang
Sneezes
T.J.'s Tree
Screech!
Christmas Shopping

SET C

Animals Love the Fair
Mr. Wind
Dad's Bike
The Grump
Buffy's Tricks
Aunt Jessie
My Monster Friends
Sally's Picture

SET D

Rain
Good-Night, Little Brother
Sleepy Bear
Mrs. Bold
Birds
BMX Billy
The Printing Machine
What Is Bat?

SET E

Just Like Grandpa
Mom's Haircut
Lilly-Lolly Little-Legs
No Extras
Scruffy Messed It Up
Green Eyes
The Surprise
Pancakes for Supper

MY MONSTER
FRIENDS

Written by Patrick Prince   Illustrated by Lorraine Ellis

Written by **Patrick Prince**
Illustrated by **Lorraine Ellis**
Designed by **Hill Graphics**

© 1989 Mimosa Publications Pty Limited

Licensed exclusively in the United States to Reed Publishing (USA) Inc.

1996 1995 1994 1993
12 11 10 9 8 7 6

Literacy 2000 is a Trademark registered in the United States Patent
and Trademark Office

Distributed in the United States of America by
RIGBY
P.O. Box 797
Crystal Lake, IL 60039-0797
800-822-8661

Distributed in Canada by
GINN PUBLISHING CANADA INC.
3771 Victoria Park Avenue
Scarborough
Ontario MIW 2P9

Printed in Hong Kong
ISBN 0 7327 0071 X